T0143908

My Island Home

PENELOPE ANN SMITH-CARTER DICHIERA

To order additional copies of this book, contact:
Xlibris
AU TFN: 1 800 844 927 (Toll Free inside Australia)
AU Local: 0283 108 187 (+61 2 8310 8187 from outside Australia)
www.xlibris.com.au
Orders@Xlibris.com.au

ISBN: Softcover   978-1-7960-0434-2
               EBook   978-1-7960-0435-9

Print information available on the last page

Rev. date: 04/19/2021

My Island Home

PENELOPE ANN SMITH-CARTER DICHIERA

When I was six nearly seven
I travelled to a place
A long way from my birth home
England.

A place so
Hot and sunny
Where the sea was
Crystal blue and a
Magical playground.

Dark night
Lit by the moon
Dreams fill
My head
Snoring,
Sleep walking.

No place
No moment
No time
Only in my sleep.
I'm the dream Queen
An imaginary space
A creation of my
mind.

Angel healing
Nightmares
Leaving.

I like to ride my new red bike
and wait for dad to finish work.

A bumpy road connected the island to the mainland.
It had been washed away by a storm
called a Cyclone.

Silence
Sea snakes
Sailboats
Sand
Sitting
Waiting
Pirate plans
Spades, buckets, dirty hands.

On weekends I loved to build cubbies and
make sandcastles with my imaginary friends,
out of the yellow sand that glistened
in the sunlight.

Rome, London, Paris France.
Taxi Cabs,
Ringing phones
Coffee pad's
Zoo's and School's
Hotel rooms and fashion fads.

I loved to read books
and learn about the places
I had never been and never seen.

Reach for the Sun, Moon and Stars,
so close yet so far.
The elements of our existence.
Weathered by time
Examples of Beauty
Science and Fantasy.

On Saturday mornings
I would go to learn ballet
on the mainland. In the
afternoon I would play
Cowboys and Indian's.
Fun laughter
Would fill me after.

Sometimes after school
I would play dress ups at my friends
house until it was time to go
home for dinner.

Match maker
Match maker
LA, LA, LA !!
Dress ups
Music, Drama
DA, DA, DA !!
"Oh, I hear mum
calling Penelope dinner time!"

Cinema nights were
the highlight of the week.
Laying back in the colourful
canvas deckchairs watching the
Milky Way.

On Sundays it was family day.
We would all stay home
mum would sew, dad would
read his newspaper or favourite book.
Chris my big sister would dance to
the latest songs.
Fred my brother made model toys and I
would draw and paint what I had seen
the day before.

Mother, Father, Sister,
Brother.
Tabby cat.

Swish goes the wind
Sway goes the rain
Bang goes our dust bin!
Meowwww goes the cat
that's the end of that !!

On school days we travelled
with a big yellow school bus
along the bumpy road,
singing to pass the time
away...

Laughter, weeping
Crying, beating, screaming
Scratching.
Paper sheeting, throwing pencils.
Naughty children!
Angry bus drivers voice
SCREAMING.....
"Sit down boys and girls!!"

My Island Home
A place to live, a place to dream, a place
like no one had ever seen.
My Island Home in the
middle of the sea, crabs and turtles, starfish
and palm trees.
Boats, bridges, sharks,
jellyfish, Mermaid Queens.
That's My Island Home.

The End

About the Author

Penelope was born in England in 1959. When she was six nearly seven her family immigrated to Perth Western Australia. A new start in a new country, arriving on the 11th of November 1965 at Perth International Airport.

In 1966 the Smith-Carter family moved to the North West of Western Australia called Finucane Island. It was a township where workers and their families lived close by. Cranking machine's crushed iron ore that had been transported by train from a mine called Goldsworthy. The Iron ore was loaded into ship's that had travelled from around the world, China, Japan and South Korea just to name a few and shipped back to their countries to be made into steel.

Finucane Island was a world away from the one Penelope had known. It was very hot and sunny the roads and houses were covered in purple dust from the iron ore. To Penelope it was a place to explore, imagine and play game's. New people arrived frequently, some left after a few months and some stayed for many years.

Penelope has always loved to draw and paint her adventures and memories of her life. Her new Country has inspired her poetry and art and the story "My Island Home". Penelope believes to indulge in your imagination is precious and the most wonderful adventure of all.

Printed in the United States
by Baker & Taylor Publisher Services